*To Cousin Andrew
and Young John,
with love*

A special thanks to Elsha Leventis, the librarians at the Oakville Public Library, the Sheridan College Library, and the University of Windsor Library for their help in producing this book.

Other books in the Discovering Canada series:

The Vikings

The Fur Traders

New France

The Defenders

DISCOVERING CANADA

Native Peoples

ROBERT LIVESEY & A.G. SMITH

Stoddart

First published in 1993 by
Stoddart Publishing Co. Limited
34 Lesmill Road
Toronto, Canada
M3B 2T6
(416) 445-3333

Third printing October 1996

CANADIAN CATALOGUING IN PUBLICATION DATA

Livesey, Robert, 1940–
    Native Peoples

(Discovering Canada)
Includes index.
ISBN 0-7737-5602-7

1. Native peoples – Canada – Juvenile literature.
 I. Smith, A.G. (Albert Gray), 1945–   .   II. Title.
III. Series: Livesey, Robert, 1940–   .   Discovering Canada

E78.C2L58 1993   j971'.00497   C93-094995-1

TEXT ILLUSTRATIONS: A.G. Smith
COVER ILLUSTRATION: A.G. Smith
COVER DESIGN: Brant Cowie/ArtPlus Limited

Printed in Canada

Stoddart Publishing gratefully acknowledges the support of the Canada Council, Ontario Ministry of Culture, Tourism, and Recreation, Ontario Arts Council, and Ontario Publishing Centre in the development of writing and publishing in Canada.

Contents

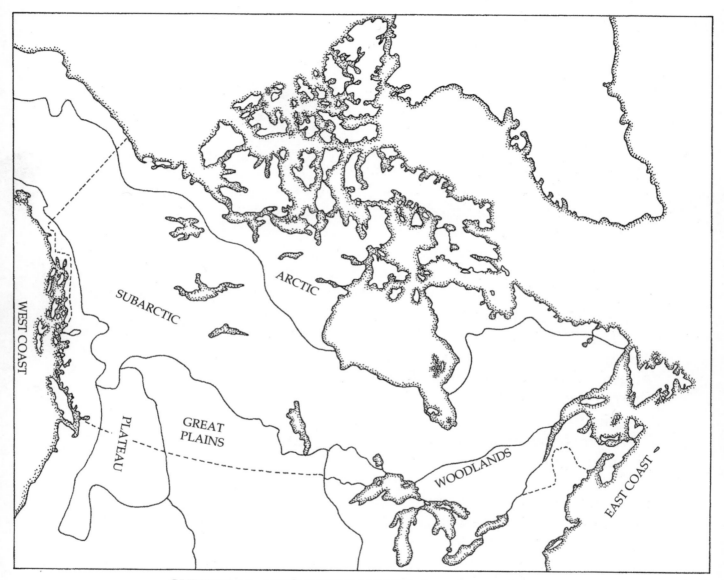

CULTURAL AREAS OF CANADA'S NATIVE PEOPLES

Introduction

Let's take an imaginary trek across Canada and discover what it was like when only the native people lived here.

If you had arrived in what is now Canada before any of the white explorers or settlers from Europe came here, you would have found numerous native communities with different customs and ways of life. Each guarded its territory and followed its own traditions.

One interesting way to get to know other people is to listen to the stories they tell about the world in which they live. As we cross the continent and meet the different groups, we will also learn some of the legends about unusual animals, famous heroes, and supernatural gods that they told their children as they huddled around camp fires in the evenings.

The first people came to North America by way of Alaska about 30,000 years ago when a bridge of land still joined this continent to Asia. Over many centuries the early wanderers slowly spread south and settled in different regions of Canada, as well as the United States, Mexico, and South America. They adapted to the new climates and environments in which they settled, and thus the life styles and traditions of the different tribes varied drastically according to the world around them. They lived very close to nature and depended on the animals and plants of their area for food, clothing, shelter, and transportation.

CHAPTER 1

People of the Rising Sun

The Giant Glooscap

How was the world created? How did humans come to exist here? Your answers to these questions will likely fall into two categories: religion or science. Before the arrival of Europeans, the native people had their own religions and stories to explain creation. The following legend was believed by the Wabanaki people:

In the beginning, before there were animals or people, the world was made of thick forests and deep waters. From a place high in the sky came Glooscap, a giant, bronze-skinned warrior who was twice as large and powerful as ordinary men. He wore a magic belt that gave him awesome powers, which he used only for good. He was half god and half man.

Glooscap paddled in his canoe to the east coast of North America, where the sun rises from the ocean every morning. There he secured his canoe to the ocean's floor and transformed it into a large, stony island decorated with tall trees. He called the island Uktamkoo; today we call it Newfoundland.

Then Glooscap shot arrows into the trunks of ash trees, and the first strong men and graceful women emerged from the trees. Glooscap named these people with golden brown skin and shining black hair the Wabanaki, which means "people of the rising sun."

Ableegumooch

Kitpou

Later, the Wabanaki journeyed from Uktamkoo and spread into the eastern forests where they formed tribes such as the Micmac, Abnaki (Abenaki), Malecite, Passamaquoddy, and Penobcot . . . but wherever they settled, they were known as Glooscap's People.

The great chief, Glooscap, ruled with love and wisdom. He taught his people how to make river dams to catch the fish, how to use the plants for medicine, and how to build birchbark wigwams and canoes.

Next, Glooscap picked up some clay and shaped it into animals, such as Ableegumooch, the Rabbit; Kitpou, the Eagle; Lusifee, the Wild Cat; Miko, the Squirrel; Mooin, the Bear; Team, the Moose; and many others.

Glooscap had a twin brother named Malsum who had travelled with him from the sky; Malsum had the face of a wolf and the body of a man. He was jealous of Glooscap and used his magic powers to do evil. While Glooscap was creating the animals, Malsum uttered an evil charm and the clay in Glooscap's hands fell to the earth where it turned into a supernatural creature that was part beaver, part badger, and part wolverine. It could take the shape of any one of those three animals.

Miko

Lusifee

Malsum smiled and announced with glee:

"Lox shall be his name!"

Glooscap agreed, but reluctantly, because he knew that Lox, like Malsum, was evil.

Originally, Glooscap had made the animals in giant forms towering over the humans. The cunning Lox went to each of the creatures and tricked it into attacking the people. When Glooscap learned of this mischief, he chased Lox away, but the sly animal still roams the land, causing trouble and tempting people and animals to do evil.

Finally, Glooscap shrunk the animals down to their present sizes and declared:

"I made the animals to be the friends of my people, but instead they attacked them. As punishment the animals shall become my people's servants, providing them with food and clothing."

Kespeadooksit . . . the story ends.

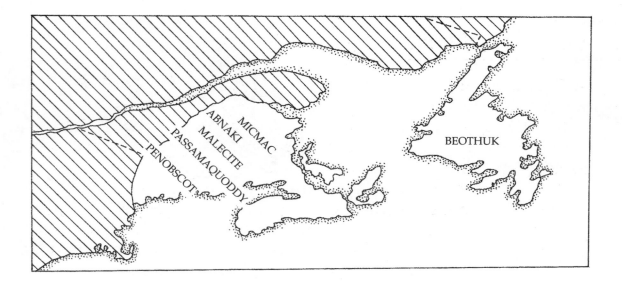

Tribes of the East Coast

There were once two main groups of natives on the east coast of Canada. The larger group spoke the Algonquian language and included such tribes as the Micmacs, Malecite, Abnaki, Penobscot, and Passamaquoddy.

The second group lived on the island of Newfoundland. Although originally from the Algonquian group, the mysterious Beothuks had developed their own unique language and culture over thousands of years of isolation from the mainland. They painted their bodies, weapons, and clothing with a paste that they created by mixing red ochre with oil. The coating protected them from cold winters and summer insects, and they believed that it had magical, life-giving power. It was this red coating that caused early settlers to call natives "redskins."

A Beothuk house was called a *mamateek.* In the interior of New-foundland several families lived together in sturdy six- or eight-sided mamateeks. These 6.6-metre homes were built in clusters, similar to houses in a suburb, where 100 to 150 people worked and hunted together.

In the summer the inland villages were deserted, like ghost towns, because the natives moved to the seaside, where they lived in smaller family groups. The summer mamateeks held six to ten people and could be constructed in less than an hour, an important feature since the hunters were frequently changing location.

MICMAC BONE DICE

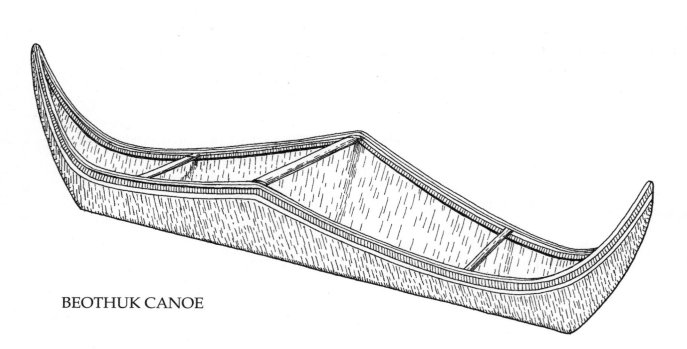

BEOTHUK CANOE

Beothuk Canoes

Beothuk canoes were different from all other native canoes. The frames were constructed from spruce, covered with birchbark, and painted with red ochre. They had keels and straight sides rather than rounded bottoms; they also curved high at both ends as well as in the middle to prevent rough ocean waves from overturning them. A Beothuk canoe ranged in length from 4.3 to 6.7 metres and held four to eight passengers.

Micmac Canoes

Micmac seagoing canoes measured 5.5 to 6.1 metres in length and 89 to 115 cm in width. The "rough-water" canoe often used between 5 and 10 square metres of sail. The Micmac would close in the bow and stern to prevent large waves from flooding the canoe, and use a long pole-handle paddle to steer or propel it. The canoe's frame would be covered with birchbark, while the paddles would usually be carved from maple.

Canada's National Sport

One legend about Glooscap describes a contest that he had with Winpe, the Wizard of the Northern Sea. They played a game of Winpe's called *tokhonon* in which each player tried to hit a stuffed moosehide ball between the opponent's goal posts with webbed sticks. After he defeated Winpe, Glooscap claimed the game as his prize and brought it back to his people. Today it is the national sport of Canada; we call it lacrosse. To prepare for a game, the natives would pray and go without food for long periods of time.

The Warning

Glooscap taught the men to make weapons, such as stone-tipped spears and bows and arrows for hunting, and showed the women how to cook meat and make clothing from animal hides. But the great chief warned his people:

"Never kill for pleasure; hunt only what you need for food and clothing! If you disobey my wishes, a giant named Famine will come to make you suffer hunger and die."

2 *Clans of the Longhouse*

Sky Woman

Are you a peaceful person? Do you have friends or classmates who like to bully or fight? The native people knew how foolish it was to fight and how much wiser it was to live in harmony with others. The tribes of the Eastern Woodlands used to tell their children the following story:

Long ago in the Sky World there was neither night nor day. Near the longhouse of the powerful Sky Chief grew the Great Tree of Light, which threw brilliant beams throughout the heavens. The people who lived there received warmth and wisdom from the tree and lived in harmony.

When the chief married a young maiden called Mature Flowers, the Fire Dragon of Jealousy captured his mind. One day the chief uprooted the Great Tree of Light and invited his bride to look down through the hole in the sky. As she leaned over the hole, he pushed her and she began to fall.

Below, there was only water. The creatures of the air and water saw Sky Woman falling toward them and came to her rescue. The birds caught her on their wings. The water creatures tried to dive to the depth of the sea and bring back mud from the bottom so that she would have a place to rest. Finally Muskrat was successful. Beaver

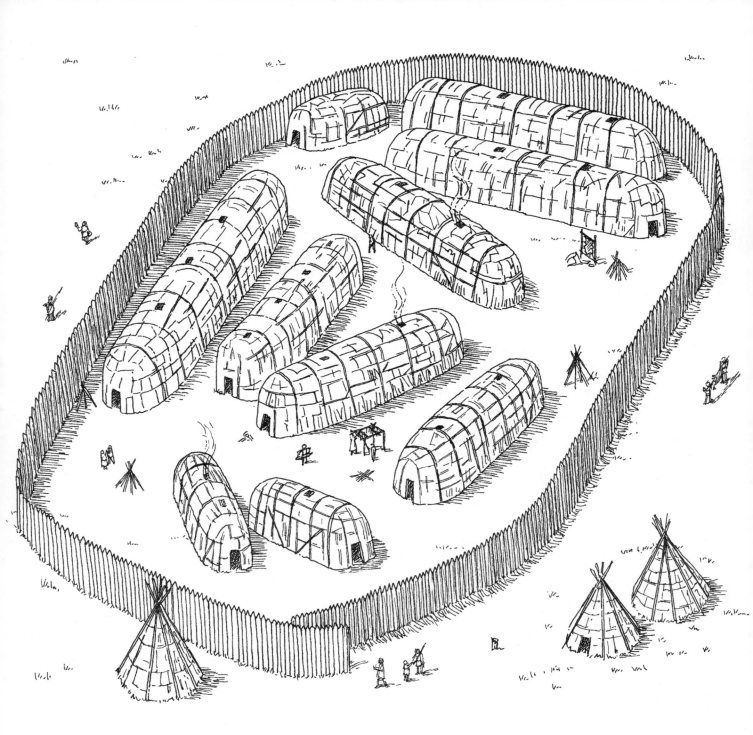

spread the mud on the back of Turtle, and the birds gently lowered Sky Woman onto the small island the animals had made. Immediately, the island began to grow. As Sky Woman explored her expanding world, seeds from her clothing dropped to the ground, and instantly plants grew up.

After the world had expanded to its present size, Sky Woman gave birth to a female child. When the child grew older, she married West Wind, who had the power to change into human form, and gave birth to twin sons. The eldest twin, who was handsome and gentle, was called Tijuskeha, or Good-Minded; the younger brother, who was ugly and cruel, was named Tawiskarong, or Flint. This evil twin deliberately caused the death of his mother, but from her grave grew the Three Sisters: Squash, Corn, and Beans. Because of this, she was then called Earth Mother.

Good-Minded received the power to create. He first created plants, animals, and songbirds and then a man in his own image whom he called Sapling and a woman he named Growing Flower. He also made rivers that ran both ways, for ease of travel.

The jealous Flint tried to imitate his brother, but his creations turned out to be serpents, thorns, thistles, bats, and monsters. In the rivers he made rapids and waterfalls that caused the rivers to flow in only one direction. To destroy the crops, Flint invented winter; however, when he challenged Good-Minded to a duel, the evil Flint was defeated and banished from the earth.

After commanding his people to live in peace with one another, Good-Minded left to live in the Sky World.

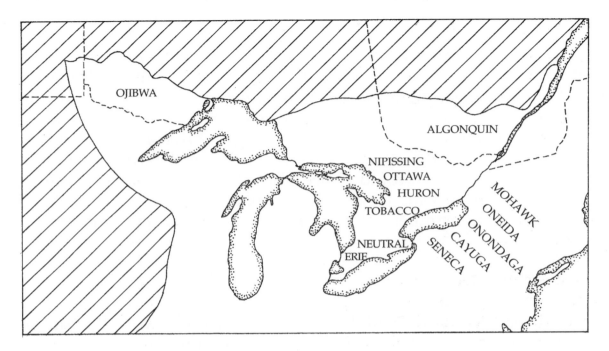

Tribes of the Woodlands

The Iroquois nation included such tribes as the Cayuga, Oneida, Onondaga, Seneca, and Mohawk, who lived along the St. Lawrence River and south of Lake Ontario. To the north of the lake, in present-day Ontario, lived their enemies the Wendots, who would later be named the Huron, Tobacco, Erie, and Neutral tribes. The Woodland natives all spoke a similar language and followed many of the same traditions. They lived in large longhouses and honoured their women, especially those who had babies. It was the mothers who elected the tribal chiefs and who could replace them if they did not approve of their behaviour. All children, male or female, belonged to the family or clan of their mother.

False Face Society

The Iroquois had many societies, or clubs; one was called the False Face Society, whose job was to scare away the Evil Spirit that caused people to become ill. Members wore large, ugly masks carved from wood and carried rattles that were usually turtle shells filled with small stones. They would dance around the sick person, chanting, rattling, and blowing ashes over the patient. If people were cured, they became members of the False Face Society and carved their own masks.

Husk Masks

The members of the Husk Face Society braided or wove their masks from corn husks. They were the ones who knew how to plant and harvest the corn, beans, and squash. To ensure good crops, they would dance with the husk masks covering their faces. These were also called "bushy head" or "fuzzy hair" masks. The members of the Husk Face Society, who could also cure the sick, carried wooden staffs to protect themselves from evil and spoke only in whispers.

The Three Sisters

The women looked after the longhouse and did the farming. The three main crops were squash, beans, and corn, which were known as The Three Sisters or Our Supporters.

FALSE FACE MASK

CORN HUSK MASK

17

Man Eaters and Rattlesnakes

The Mohawks were mighty warriors, feared by their enemies. They called themselves Ganiengehaka, which means People of the Flint Country, but their opponents called them Mowak (Mohawk), which means Man Eaters. Likewise, the Iroquois called themselves Hodenosaunee, which means People of the Longhouse. It was their enemy, the Algonquins, who named them Iroquois, which is an insulting name that means Rattlesnake.

Longhouses

The Woodland people lived in villages of longhouses, which were narrow buildings 15 to 45 metres long and 5.5 to 7.5 metres wide. They had no windows, and their arched roofs were covered with strips of elm bark. Inside lived families or clans descended from a "clan mother," who was the eldest female member of the family. A sign over the doorway indicated the clan to which the people belonged. For example: a turtle, a bear, a beaver, a wolf, etc.

The Hiawatha Belt

This belt was made to celebrate the founding of the League of Peace. The pine tree in the centre represents the Onondaga territory where the Five Nations held their meetings, while the rectangles symbolize the other four tribes. The original belt is on display at the New York State Museum in Albany.

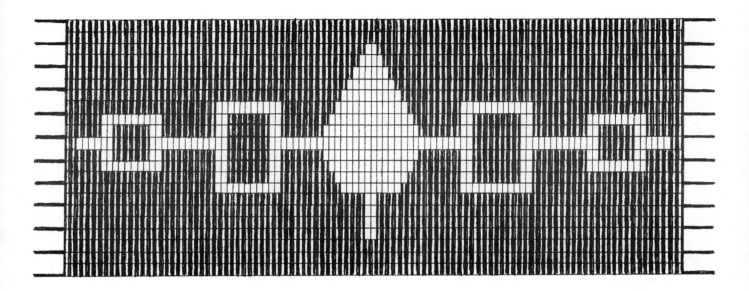

The Great Tree of Peace

Long ago, the Iroquois chief Deganawidah had a vision. He and the famous Hiawatha persuaded the chiefs of the Seneca, Cayuga, Onondaga, Oneida, and Mohawk to join in a Five Nations alliance that invited all tribes to live together in peace. Later, the Tuscaroras, who were pushed out of North Carolina by the whites, became the sixth nation. The Iroquois called their confederacy the Great Tree of Peace, whose branches offered protection and whose roots stretched throughout the land, where anyone was welcome to grab hold of them and discover peace.

Each tribe elected members, called *sachems*, to a central government. Later the English and the Ojibway became partners, and the conquered Hurons and Erie were also welcomed into the alliance.

Build a Longhouse

The Iroquois and their neighbours of the Eastern Woodlands lived in longhouses. They were built of a framework of poles tied together and covered with birch or elm bark.

What You Need:
scissors
white glue such as Elmer's
a blunt-edged scoring tool such as a table knife
paper

What to Do*:

1. Cut out the two end pieces and the large side and roof piece.

2. Score along the edge of the tabs and fold them back.

3. Apply glue to the long tab on one side of each of the end pieces and attach one side of the wall to both ends.

4. After the glue on these tabs has dried, continue the process with the short tabs around the top of the ends and the other long tabs on the other side. If you copy the pages, you and your friends can arrange several longhouses to form a village.

* You may photocopy or trace these five pages

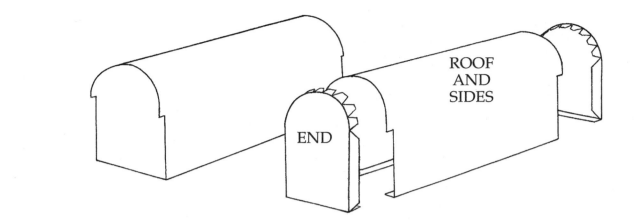

ROOF
AND
SIDES

END

END
PIECES

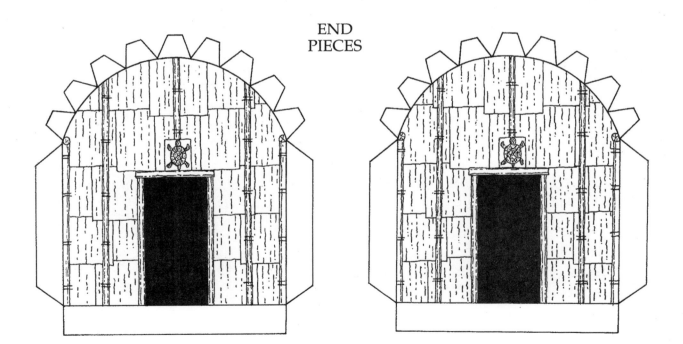

21

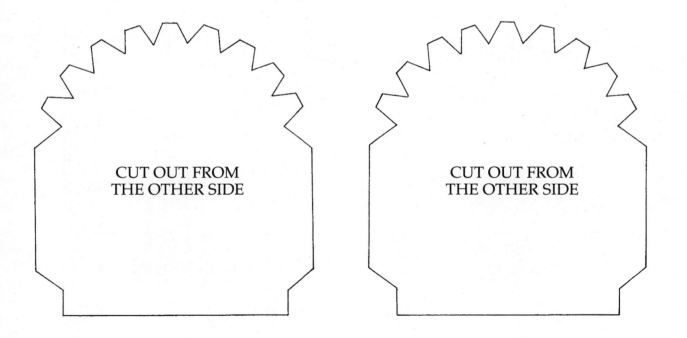

CUT OUT FROM
THE OTHER SIDE

CUT OUT FROM
THE OTHER SIDE

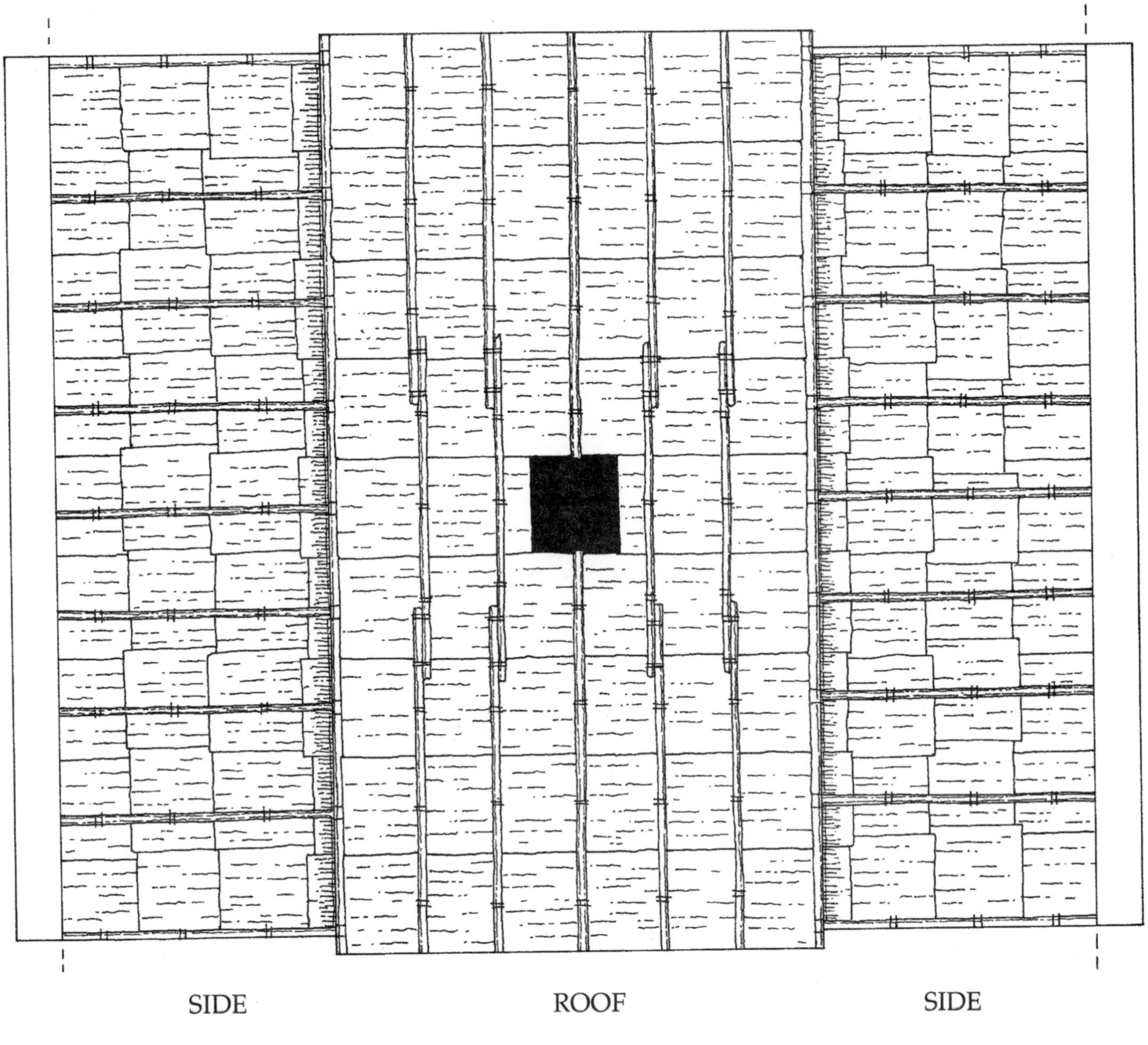
SIDE
ROOF
SIDE

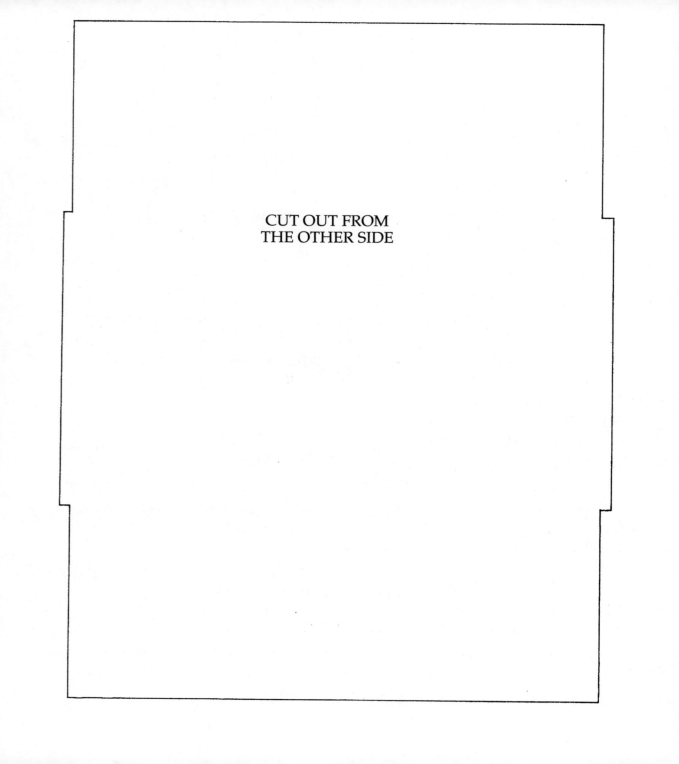

CUT OUT FROM
THE OTHER SIDE

Dream Guessing (Native Psychology)

The Woodland natives believed that unconscious desires caused mental anguish and were revealed by people's dreams. To cure unhappiness, the dream wish had to be recognized and satisfied.

Part of their religious rituals during the Midwinter Festival involved the practice of guessing what an unhappy person had dreamed about. The dreamer would offer clues with mime actions or by singing, dancing, or shouting. The others would have to guess the dreamer's wish, then satisfy it. Once the dreamers had obtained their wishes, their minds were healed and they became happy and content. It was considered dishonest to invent a dream for personal gain. If a dream wish was too great or too hostile to be rewarded in reality, it was fulfilled through playacting.

Talking Beads (Wampum Belts)

Wampum belts told the history of the tribe as well as recording its laws and customs. Wampum beads were made from seashells: white wampum from the inside of a conch or whelk, purple wampum from a saltwater clam. Each tribe had an official Keeper of the Wampum, who memorized the visual and symbolic stories of each belt and passed them on to a young apprentice who would one day become the next Keeper. Wampum belts were considered sacred and, because the Woodland people had no books or written words, they were the only recorded history of the tribe. After the arrival of the white man, wampum was used like money to bargain or trade for European goods.

3 *Nomads of the Trail*

Wisakedjak

A young member of a Cree band travelling the northern forest trails in search of food would have been told stories about Wisakedjak, whose mischief caused problems for both humans and animals. The following legend was entertaining, as well as a warning about how to behave:

After the Creator had made the world and all the creatures, he placed Wisakedjak in charge and told him to look after the land and teach the people and animals how to live together in peace. But Wisakedjak allowed them to do as they wished, and soon they were fighting and killing one another.

The angry Creator warned Wisakedjak to stop the useless bloodshed, but he did not obey. Instead, he played tricks on the people and animals, causing them to become more violent and disobedient. The earth turned red from the blood.

Again the Creator scolded Wisakedjak and warned that he would destroy them all and wash the world clean if they did not change their behaviour . . . but the bloodshed continued.

Then came the rain. Day and night it poured down, causing the rivers and lakes to flood their banks until every living thing was drowned except for Wisakedjak, one otter, one beaver, and one tiny muskrat. Because he had supernatural powers, Wisakedjak sat on the water; Otter, Beaver, and Muskrat swam beside him.

CREE TRAPPERS

Wisakedjak was sorry for his foolishness and wept. Even when the rain stopped, he did not dare to talk to the Creator. Wisakedjak did not have the power to create, but he did have the magic to multiply what had been created. He told his animal friends that he would make an island for them to live on if one of them would bring him a bit of the old earth from beneath the water.

First, Otter tried to dive to the bottom of the flood waters, but after three tries he was exhausted and gave up. Next, Beaver made three attempts, but he, too, became tired and had to quit. Finally, the little Muskrat dove down, and on his third effort he returned with a sample of the earth between his claws.

Overjoyed, Wisakedjak grabbed the earth and expanded it into an island on which they all rested. The Creator, seeing that they were sorry, commanded the rivers to take the waters down to the ocean and re-created mankind, animals, and trees. This time he took away Wisakedjak's powers over people and animals, except the power to flatter or deceive. That is why, even today, people can be fooled by Wisakedjak and find themselves in much trouble.

28

NASKAPI DOLL

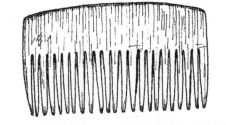

COMB WITH BIRCHBARK
CASE AND CLEANER

29

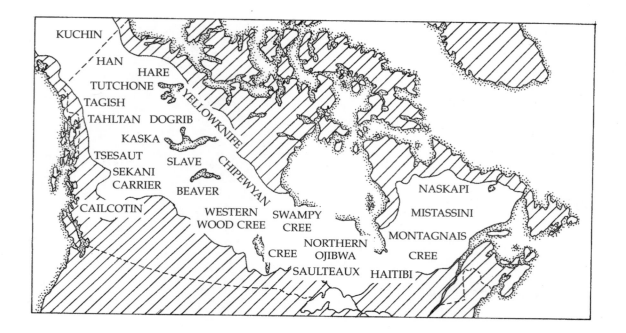

Tribes of the Subarctic

The people who lived in the cold northern forests south of the Arctic belonged to two main groups. In the northeast, they spoke dialects of the Algonquian language and included such tribes as the Naskapi, Cree, Montagnais, Northern Ojibwa, and Algonquin. In the northwest they spoke different versions of the Athapaskan language and consisted of tribes like the Kutchin, Hare, Tutchone, Kaska, Dogrib, Yellowknife, Chipewyan, Sekani, and Beaver. The animals on which the Subarctic tribes depended for food, clothing, and shelter migrated with the seasons, thus the people also became nomads, following the wild creatures from place to place.

Shamans

A shaman was a medicine man or woman who could cure sickness by using magic medicine made from plant roots and tree bark, communicate through dreams with animal spirits, and see into the future by performing the mysterious ritual known as "the shaking tent." Only a shaman knew what magic happened inside the tent.

Animal Spirits

The people of the trail believed that all animals had spirits. If Cree hunters killed a bear, they would light pipes, blow the smoke over the dead animal, and beg the angry spirit to forgive them, explaining that the kill was necessary so that they could obtain food and warm furs.

The Sacred Number

The Algonquin, as well as other tribes of the Subarctic, believed that the number four was sacred. It explained how the Great Spirit (God) created the world with four directions (north, south, east, west), four seasons (fall, winter, spring, summer) four parts of a plant (root, stem, leaf, flower), and so on.

Windigo

The Windigo was a powerful evil spirit that caused problems for and did harm to people.

Bone Maps

Naskapi natives used a ceremony known as "scapulomancy," during which they placed bones in a sacred fire. After the fire had cooled, they read the cracks in the bones to learn where the herds were and what trails to take.

Real or Uncivilized?

Napskapi natives called themselves Nanenot, which meant "true, real men"; their enemies, the Montagnais, called them Naskapi, which meant "rude, uncivilized people." The Montagnais, who lived in the Laurentian Mountains to the south, in turn received their name from early French settlers; it comes from *montagne*, which means mountains. The French also labelled the Athapaskan tribe we now call Slave with the term *esclave*, since their neighbours, the Cree, would go on raiding parties to bring back captives.

Native English

In Canada we use many traditional native words when we speak the English language today. Some examples are moose, moccasins, chipmunk, pemmican, muskeg, and toboggan.

Snow Shoes

Trail people used round-shaped bear-paw or beaver-tail snowshoes for soft, deep snow and long, narrow ones with pointed ends for hard, frozen snow.

CARIBOU

Hunting the Herds

Using spears or bows and arrows, the hunters of the trail followed herds of larger animals through the thick Subarctic forests. Many Algonquians searched for moose; northern people hunted caribou such as the one shown above; southern tribes tracked deer. They used traps or snares to catch smaller game like beaver or rabbit.

Cree Moccasin Game

This is a hiding and guessing game. It requires quick hands and sharp eyes! Many native peoples across North America from the Arctic to the American Southwest played similar games.

What You Need:
four small balls, marbles, or stones of the same size (three of them should be of one colour; the fourth a different colour)
four moccasins (sneakers or pieces of cloth shaped like moccasins will work fine)
a stick about a half metre to one metre long

What to Do:

1. This game is played by two people. The first player hides each of the four balls under a moccasin as the other player watches. Be very careful that the player watching does not detect under which moccasin the odd-coloured ball has been placed.

2. The second player then must guess under which moccasin the odd-coloured ball is hidden.

3. The stick is used to turn over the moccasins so there can be no last minute sleight of hand.

4. The second player now hides the balls, and the play continues.

5. The first player to reach a pre-determined number, say five or ten, of correct guesses is the winner.

FOUR BALLS

MOCCASINS AND STICK

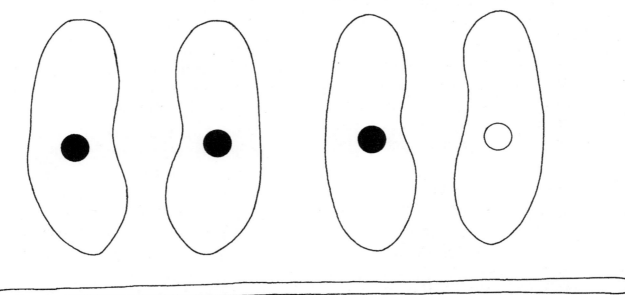

4 *Inuit of the North*

Father Raven

Imagine what it would have been like to live in the dark, frozen Arctic in the days before modern inventions. The Inuit say no one knows for certain about the beginning or the end of life; we are born from darkness and return to it when we die. The following is the story told by the old people:

Tulungersaq awoke suddenly in darkness. He stretched out his arms and groped in the dark, but his fingers found only dead clay. Then he touched his face and felt his nose, eyes, and mouth; he was a human being . . . as we are today. On his forehead he discovered a mysterious knot and wondered why it was there. In the dark he found a hard object on the ground and instinctively buried it.

Exploring his surroundings, he crawled cautiously over the cold clay until he stopped at the side of a cliff. He tossed a hunk of clay into the empty space below and listened for it to land, but he heard nothing. As he turned to leave, there was a whirring in his ears, and something soft landed on his hand. He gently caressed the tiny creature and found a beak, feathers, and small clawed feet. It was a sparrow.

Returning to where he had buried the object, he discovered that it had grown roots and the clay was now alive with grass and bushes. Tulungersaq felt lonely and, using the clay, shaped a figure in his

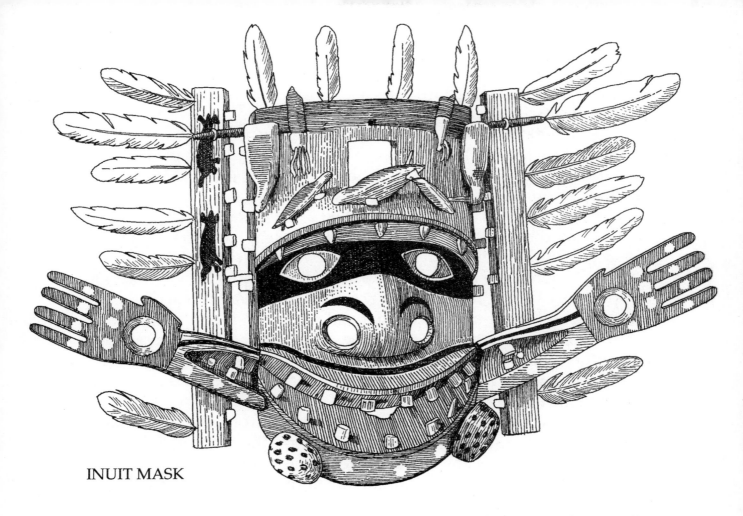

INUIT MASK

own likeness. It came alive instantly and started digging frantically in the earth. But the creature was not like him . . . it was bad-tempered and destructive. Realizing his error, Tulungersaq dragged it to the edge of the cliff and threw it into the abyss. Later this creature became Tornaq, the evil spirit that plagues the earth.

The sparrow became Tulungersaq's constant companion and often sat on his shoulder. Curious about the abyss, he sent the sparrow to

37

explore it, and when the bird returned, it told him that new land was forming below.

Determined to see for himself, Tulungersaq made wings out of twigs and fastened them to his shoulders. To his surprise, they transformed into real wings and he felt himself growing feathers. The mysterious knot on his forehead grew into a beak; he became a large, black bird that could fly. He called himself Raven.

He flew from the darkness that he called Heaven to the bottom of the abyss, which he called Earth. There he created new herbs and flowers. When large pods grew up, he opened one of them and out popped a beautiful human being, fully grown. Astonished, Raven threw back his bird mask and changed back into human form himself, happily greeting the newcomer. Then other humans emerged from other pods.

"When I planted these pods, I didn't know what would come out of them," he admitted.

Later, a large black sea monster emerged from the ocean, and Raven helped the humans kill it. They cut up the carcass and threw the parts around, causing all the large Arctic islands to form. Slowly, the Earth grew and became a home for humans and other creatures. Raven called his people together and declared:

"I am your Father and creator . . . you must never forget me!"

Finally, Raven flew back to the dark Heaven, but first he threw firestones into the sky, creating light on Earth.

DRUM DANCER

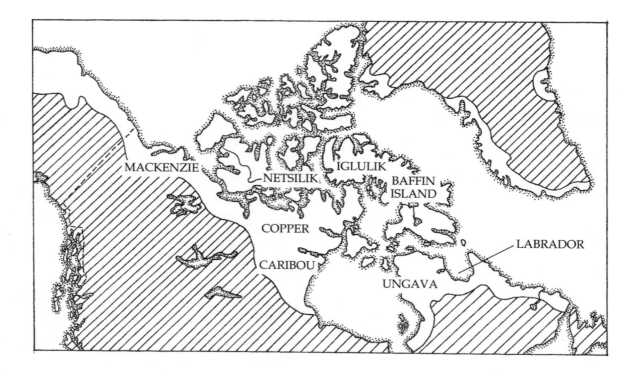

Tribes of the North

The people who lived in the Arctic had to be strong and rugged to survive the freezing weather and harsh living conditions. Their main foods were meat and blubber. The latter was necessary because without fat the Inuit could not have survived in such a cold climate. There were fourteen major tribes spread across the North, four in Alaska, eight in Canada, and two in Greenland. Recently, the Canadian government has recognized Inuit land rights and agreed to establish a new territory to allow them self-government. The Canadian Inuit tribes were the Mackenzie, Copper, Caribou, Netsilik, Iglulik, Baffin Island, Labrador, and Ungava.

Dog Teams

It took six to twelve dogs to pull an Inuit sledge. Below the treeline or in the west the dogs were harnessed, with the strongest in front, in pairs or in single file because the trails were narrow. In the open northern spaces, the huskies were on separate lines and arranged in a fan-shaped pattern. The Inuit measured distances not in miles or kilometres but in "sleeps," which referred to the number of nights it took to travel a distance.

Eaters of Raw Flesh

The people of the North are often referred to as Eskimos, which was the name given to them by the natives to the south. It means "eaters of raw flesh." They prefer to be called Inuit, which is their own name meaning "the people."

INUIT IVORY
CHARM DOLL

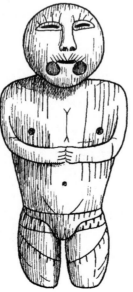

Kayaks and Umiaks

There were two types of boats used by the Inuit, the kayak and the umiak. The kayak was a thin, light craft that was designed for only one person and used mainly for hunting. It ranged from 3.5 to 6.5 metres in length and was completely covered except for a small central opening where the hunter sat with his double-bladed paddle. The umiak was a larger, ocean-going vessel that was 9 to 12 metres long and used for whaling or carrying entire families and their belongings. It sometimes would have a sail made from the intestines of seals, and would be rowed by the women when families were changing location.

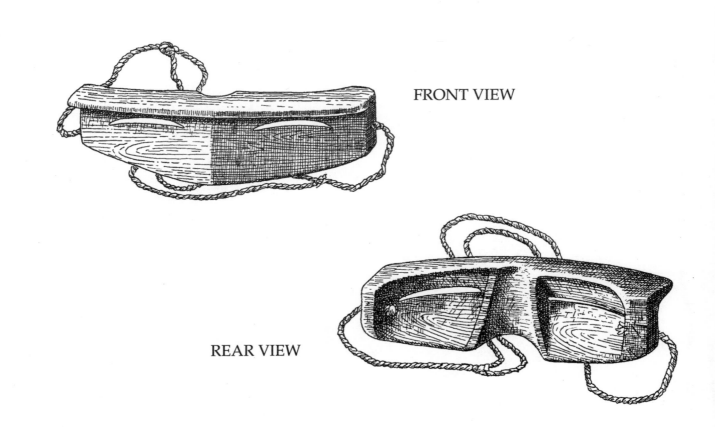

FRONT VIEW

REAR VIEW

Snow Goggles

The Inuit often wore goggles to protect their eyes from the glare of the sun on the snow. Glare was especially a problem when the sun was low in the early spring. The goggles were made from curved pieces of driftwood, carefully carved to fit over the eyes and nose. A narrow slit allowed the wearer to see. The goggles were tied around the head with sealskin cords.

EXTERIOR OF AN IGLOO

Igloo — Outside

The winter home of an Inuit was called an igloo and was built with large blocks of frozen snow in a circle, sloped upwards and inwards to form a dome-shaped roof. The last ceiling block would have a ventilation hole, and sometimes a small, semi-transparent window made of ice or seal intestine was carved in the wall of the igloo. The builder would use a saw made from an antler to cut the blocks, and a knife of ivory to trim them.

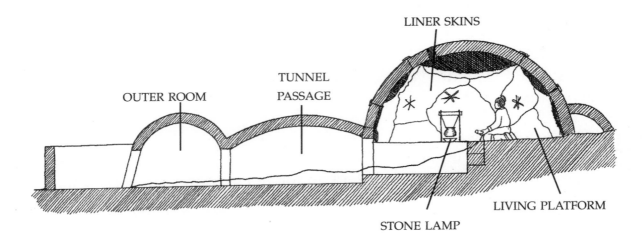

LINER SKINS

TUNNEL
PASSAGE

OUTER ROOM

LIVING PLATFORM

STONE LAMP

INTERIOR OF AN IGLOO

Igloo — Inside

The Inuit crawled into their igloos and would hang their outer fur clothing in the entrance tunnel. There was no furniture, only a large, raised snow platform on which the family slept and smaller ones that served as chairs and tables, where they ate and worked. The ceiling and walls were lined with animal skins, and the bed was covered with warm furs. Because there is very little wood in the Far North, the Inuit burned seal oil in a soapstone bowl for heat and to cook their food.

47

Play an Inuit Game

Nuglukutug is a game based on the skills needed for hunting. It was played in the igloos on long Arctic nights.

What You Need:
a long piece of string and a short piece of string
a diamond-shaped piece of wood about 12 cm long with a 4-cm hole in the centre
a piece of wood or small stone for weight
a plastic straw for each player

What to Do:
1. Tie one end of the long string to the ceiling or a tree limb and the other end through a small hole at one end of the diamond-shaped object plate.

2. Tie one end of the short string to the bottom of the object plate and the other end around the wood or stone weight. Give the weight an easy swing.

3. Two or three players sit around the suspended object plate with their straws ready. When the signal "Go!" is given, each player tries to thrust the straw through the hole. The player who is first to do so gets one point. The first player to score ten points is the winner.

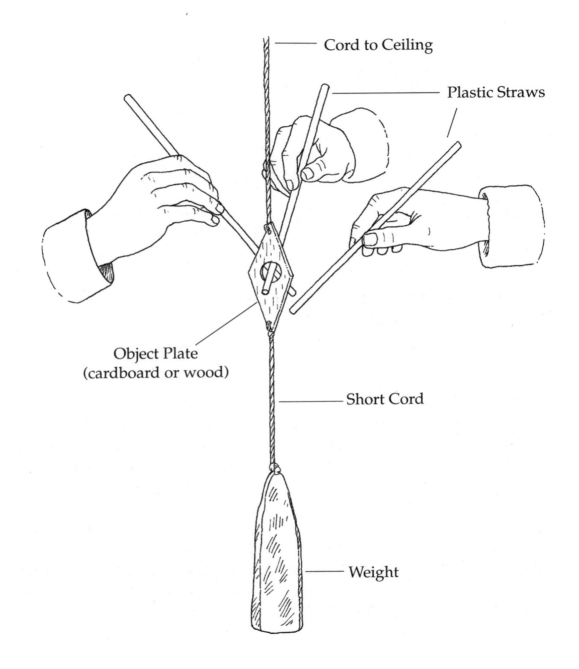

Cord to Ceiling

Plastic Straws

Object Plate
(cardboard or wood)

Short Cord

Weight

49

CHAPTER **5** *Natives of the Plains*

Thunder Man

If you had been a young Blackfoot native, huddled in your teepee during a fierce prairie thunderstorm, you likely would have heard an elder telling the following tale:

Many moons ago, three young Piegan maidens were picking wild berries when they heard a loud noise. Suddenly, the towering figure of Thunder Man, cloaked in a robe of black mink, stood before them.

"It's Thunder Man," gasped Little Sticks.

"He'll kill us," moaned Prairie Hen. "Let's run for the camp."

They tried to run to the safety of their village, but they felt the earth tremble beneath them as Thunder-Man's powerful footsteps overtook them. One of the terrified women was Blue Teal, daughter of the chief, who cried out desperately:

"I'll become your wife if you spare us!"

Hearing these words, Thunder Man shot one of his flashing arrows, which smashed loudly against a distant mountain top, and then he headed south, leaving the three shuddering women behind.

A week later, while Blue Teal was alone, gathering wood, a handsome stranger with red hair appeared in front of her.

"Who are you? What do you want?" gasped Blue Teal in fear.

50

"You promised to be my wife if I spared you," he replied as he swept her up with the wind and flew away to the Sky World.

When his daughter failed to return home, Blue Teal's father ordered his braves to search for her, but even the best scouts could find no trace. It was the young medicine man who learned the truth from a magpie. White Beaver told the chief that he would create magic to bring Blue Teal home on the condition that he could marry her. The chief agreed.

Blue Teal was well cared for in the Thunder Man's teepee. Servants supplied her with buffalo and antelope meat as well as sweet berries. Her husband brought her precious stones the colours of the rainbow, and from them she made the first necklace ever worn by a Piegan woman. But she was sad because she secretly loved White Beaver.

Then, while gathering wild turnips, Blue Teal saw one that was much larger than the others. That evening, White Beaver's magic caused Blue Teal to dream about the mother turnip. She wondered how large it was and how deep it grew. The next day she returned and started digging around it. She dug so deeply that a hole appeared in the Sky World and, below, she could see her father's camp. Then she became homesick and began to cry.

"What will make you happy again?" asked Thunder Man.

"Let me return home for just one moon," she begged.

He agreed, and when she arrived, her people rejoiced. Then White Beaver reminded the chief of his promise.

"But what will I tell Thunder Man when he returns?"

"I have strong medicine to take care of him," White Beaver assured the chief.

52

DRYING BUFFALO
MEAT

The day that Thunder Man returned for Blue Teal, White Beaver heard the ground shaking. Dressed in his medicine-man costume, he emerged from his teepee, holding a magic pipe with a black bowl decorated with four black crow's feathers. He took four puffs and blew the smoke toward the North.

Immediately, the air grew freezing cold. Thunder Man, who likes only hot weather, retreated to the South.

Thunder Man never dared to return as long as White Beaver lived. The sacred "thunder pipe" was passed on to the descendants of Blue Teal and White Beaver.

Tribes of the Plains

The natives who lived on the flat, short-grassed prairies roamed from the Rocky Mountains of Alberta to present day Manitoba and south into the American Plains. They included such tribes as the Piegan, Blood, and Gros Ventres (Big Belly), which belonged to the Blackfoot nation. This group were called Blackfoot because their moccasins were blackened by the ashes of prairie fires. The Plains Cree, Assiniboin, Ojibwa, and Sioux also inhabited parts of the Canadian Prairies.

They lived in portable teepees, which could be quickly erected or torn down as the natives followed the buffalo herds across the plains. Their weapons were bows, arrows, spears, lances, and clubs, and they were known for the colourful war bonnets and headdress worn by their chiefs and medicine men. The rare eagle feather could only be worn by one who had proven that he was brave.

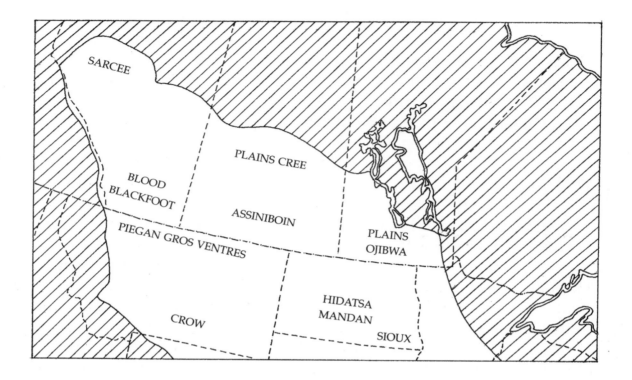

The Dog Days

The early Plains natives had only dogs to pull their belongings on sledges or travois. When the Europeans brought horses to this continent, the lives of the warriors improved. They could then hunt buffalo and battle enemy on horseback. Also, they built horse *travois* and could venture farther out onto the endless flat prairies rather than living near the rolling hills on the edge of it.

Medicine Bag

When a Plains baby was born, its navel cord was cut and placed in a decorated medicine bag. As the child grew, he or she added special or magical objects to the bag, which was often worn around the neck. The contents of the medicine bag was a secret known only to the person who wore it. The loss of the bag meant spiritual death.

Marriage

Native girls became brides at an early age, between twelve and fourteen or as soon as they were able to have a baby of their own. The young man brought gifts to the parents of the young woman, but if she objected to the marriage, her wishes were respected.

Vision Quest

When a boy went from childhood to manhood, at about thirteen years of age, he took a lone journey away from his camp during which he would not eat for several days. During that time he would pray for a vision that would direct his future life, a spirit that would come to him in a dream or trance. The spirit, sometimes that of a wild animal, might direct him to become a warrior, a chief, a medicine man, or a hunter. A young boy's name changed as he grew, depending on his behaviour; often he gained his final adult name based on the events of his vision quest.

Pipe Smoking

For the natives of the Plains, smoking was a religious ceremony, not a bad habit as it is today. Only men participated. As they sat in a circle, a warrior would fill a pipe with red willow bark and point it toward the northern sky to honour the Great Spirit. Next, he would point it east, south, west, and north again before smoking and passing it clockwise around the circle.

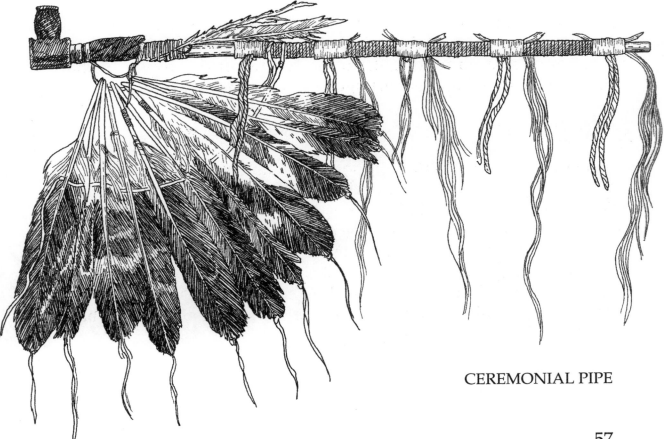

CEREMONIAL PIPE

Buffalo Jump

The Plains people depended on the buffalo for food, clothing, and teepees. When a herd of buffalo was found, the medicine man would lead the others in a dance to the Buffalo Spirit to assure a successful hunt. In the days before horses, there were two ways to hunt the buffalo. The warriors could surround the herd and creep up on the animals slowly; then, at a signal from the leader, rush forward, whooping and firing arrows. Or, they could create a stampede and force the buffalo to jump over a high cliff or riverbank. The second method could give them a supply of meat for the whole winter. Since buffalo do not fear wolves, the natives would sometimes hide under wolf skins to crawl up to the herd.

Following a successful hunt, the best portions of the meat were given to widows, orphans, and old people. The buffalo's scrotum (the scent bag) was buried to offer thanks to the Buffalo Spirit.

Plains Sign Language

The natives on the Plains spoke different languages or dialects, but they belonged to the same culture, which means that they all lived, dressed, hunted, and worshipped in a similar fashion. To communicate for purposes of trade and diplomacy, they developed a universal language of hand signs. There were over seven hundred and fifty signs. Today a sign language is used by deaf people to communicate, and referees and umpires at football, baseball, and hockey games also use a sign language.

What You Need:
your hands
a friend

What to Do:
1. On the next page are examples of hand signs. Learn these and make up others.

2. Use them to communicate with your friends. Most of them are quite logical. For instance, you may already use the sign for *big* when telling about a fish you caught. There were also signs to describe animals. What do you think the sign for *buffalo* would be? The answer is on page 89.

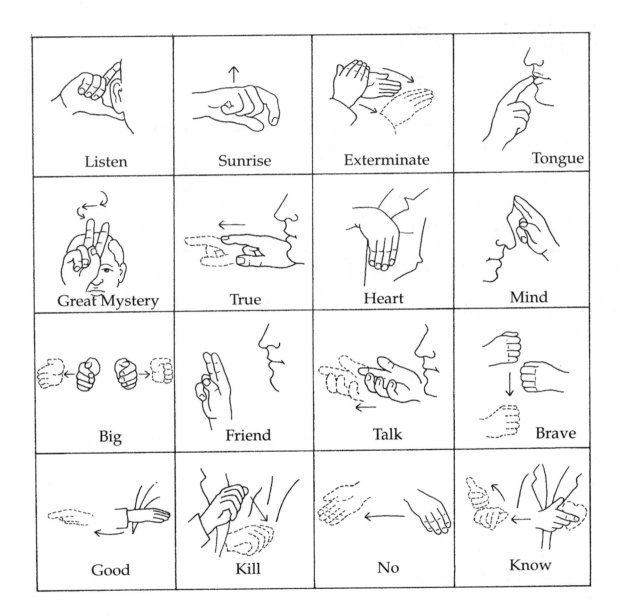

Listen	Sunrise	Exterminate	Tongue
Great Mystery	True	Heart	Mind
Big	Friend	Talk	Brave
Good	Kill	No	Know

63

Bull Boat

The people of the Plains used buffalo hides stretched over large frames of wood to build unusual-looking, round bull boats, which they paddled across prairie rivers or lakes.

Powwow

The Plains natives belonged to societies, or clubs, of warriors, medicinemen, hunters, dog soldiers (policemen), and others. A young person was born into a society but, if sponsored, could join another by studying under a teacher and learning the secrets and rituals involved. Special ceremonies, powwows, were times when members met to sing, dance, visit, share sacred vows, offer prayers of thanksgiving, or ask for guidance. Even today, some of the secrets of the powwow are still unknown to nonmembers.

Counting Coup

Plains warriors believed that riding close to their enemies and touching them with a coup stick was a greater victory than killing them. They would count each successful blow. This custom was respected by all Plains tribes until the white man arrived. He didn't understand this game of honour and would quickly shoot a native attempting to count coup.

Sun Dance

Plains natives believed that the sun was the origin of all life. On special occasions a warrior would cut down a thin tree and replant it in the centre of camp. To prove his bravery, he would insert wooden hooks into his chest and attach leather thongs to them, which he would then tie to the tree. As the morning sun came up, he would dance around the tree in a trance until the hooks were pulled from his body. The warrior would later display the scars with pride.

6 *Plateau People*

Coyote

Today, most young people watch cartoon shows about animal characters on TV or in movie theatres. Long ago, all the children of the Rocky Mountain tribes in present-day British Columbia used to be told tales about animal people. They would have known the following story about Coyote:

In the beginning, before humans came to the mountains, there were only animal people, and their leader was Coyote, the trickster, who was silly, greedy, boastful, and sly. When he heard that a river monster named Nashlah was swallowing his animal people as they paddled their canoes up the Columbia River, Coyote promised to help. But the foolish Coyote had no idea what to do until he asked his three sisters, who lived in the form of huckleberries. After hearing their advice, Coyote announced arrogantly:

"Yes, that was what I was going to do."

Following the plan of his sisters, Coyote gathered pitch, sagebrush, and dry wood, and sharpened five knives. When he approached the river monster, it did not try to swallow him because it knew that Coyote was a powerful chief. Coyote knew he would have to trick it, so he insulted, taunted, and teased Nashlah until the monster grew angry and swallowed him.

Inside the stomach of Nashlah, Coyote discovered many cold and hungry animal people who had been victims of the monster. Using the

pitch and wood, Coyote made a fire to warm his animal friends. Then he started to cut out the monster's heart to cook for them. But as he hacked at the tough cord that held the heart to the body of the monster, the first, second, third, and fourth knives broke. Finally, using the fifth knife, Coyote cut through the last strand, and the entire heart fell into the fire.

The monster uttered a loud roar and coughed up Coyote and his animal friends. Then Coyote gave each of the creatures a name, such as Deer, Owl, Beaver, Salmon, Cougar, Woodpecker, and Bear. Also he made a new rule for the monster.

"A new race of humans will come soon," he declared, "They must be allowed to travel up and down the river. You should not swallow them, although you may shake their canoes as they pass over your house."

Since that day, Nashlah rarely overturns canoes and swallows people. Usually, humans take their canoes out of the river and carry them around the deep, swirling waters where Nashlah still lives.

Tribes of the Mountains

In the heart of Canada's majestic Rocky Mountains a variety of tribes lived on the forested plateaus or in the lush valley havens protected by tall, snow-capped mountains. They travelled the fast-flowing rivers that cut through narrow rocky canyons, splashed against jagged rocks, and flowed over foaming falls. Tribes such as the Lillooet, Ntlakyapamuk, Thompson, Kootenay, Shuswap, Okanagan, Nicola, Lake, Interior Salish, Carrier, and Chilcotin enjoyed an abundance of berries, fish, and wildlife. They traded with the people of the Pacific Coast, the Great Plains and the Subarctic, often adapting life-styles and ideas from each.

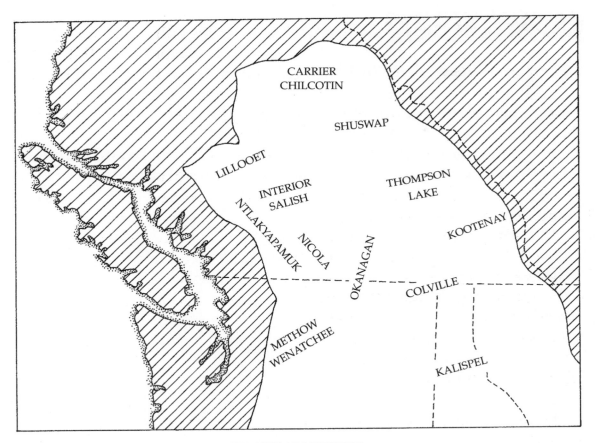

PLATEAU TRIBES

Invent a Native Nickname

Native children's names changed as they grew, and usually described their personalities, behaviour, or achievements; frequently they are associated with nature and wildlife. By twelve or fourteen, when they became adults, they chose a permanent name.

What You Need:
imagination

What to Do:
1. Invent native names for your friends, family, classmates, and yourself. The name should be one that the person likes; insulting names would show bad manners.

Here are some examples, but be original and invent your own: Thunder Voice, Singing Sparrow, White Blossom, Swift Salmon, Peace Maker, Strong Branch, Laughing Spirit, Golden Doe, Big Heart, Eagle Eyes.

COYOTE

Cliff Art

If you travel through the interior plateau of British Columbia today, you will discover mysterious native paintings on the sides of cliffs and large boulders that tell the history of the people who lived there thousands of years ago. The key to understanding these stories today has been lost, but their beauty lives on.

Native Peoples Crossword Puzzle*

ACROSS:

2. A sacred number.
4. A tribe called "uncivilized" by their enemies.
5. An Inuit measurement of distance on a long trip.
8. A party thrown by West Coast tribes to erect a totem.
10. The name of this group of natives meant "people of the rising sun."
11. A native medicine doctor.
12. A quest that native boys went on to become adults.
13. Native people who used to live in Newfoundland.
15. The animal used to pull a travois before the horse.
17. A native tribe called Man Eaters by their enemies.
18. A Plains native's house.
19. The native name for Canada's national sport.
21. Inuit houses.
23. An Inuit spearing game.
25. A powerful, evil spirit.
26. A popular food for West Coast tribes.
27. An Inuit one-person boat.
30. A Beothuk house.

* You may photocopy puzzle and clues. See page 89 for answers.

31. A belt created at the founding of the League of Peace.
32. People of the longhouse belonged to these groups.

DOWN:

1. Beaded belts used to record history and laws.
3. The native name for Newfoundland.
6. Woodland people's houses.
7. An insulting name given to Inuits.
9. An evil twin whose name meant Flint.
13. The animal that Plains natives relied on for food.
14. Visual stories built by West Coast natives.
15. An Iroquois chief who formed a Five Nations alliance.
16. A tribe called Rattlesnake by their enemies.
20. A twin whose name meant Good-Minded.
22. Who created "the people of the rising sun?"
24. An ocean-going Inuit boat.
28. The continent from which native people emigrated.
29. The bird associated with Inuit creation.

72

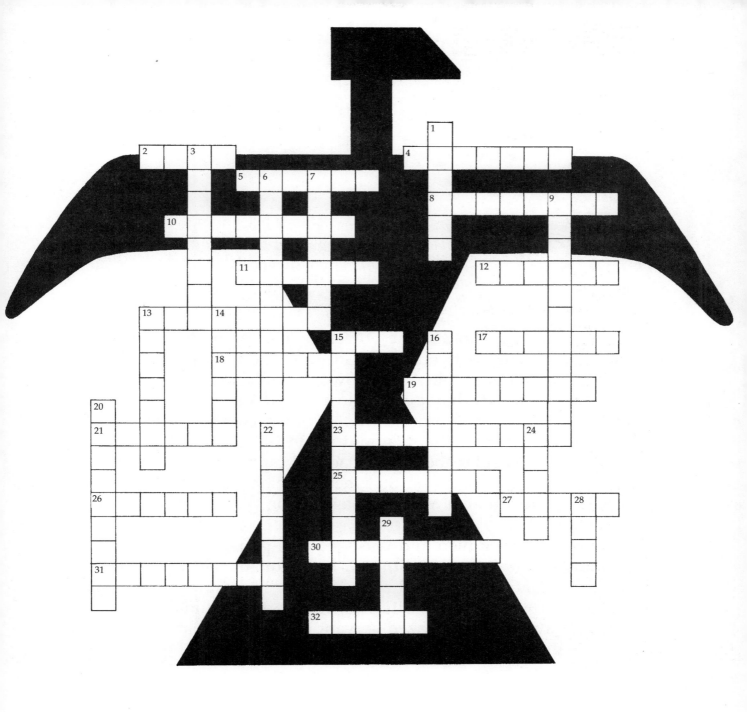

Fog Woman

Salmon was the main food for most Pacific coast tribes. If you had been a young West Coast native in present-day British Columbia, you would have read the following story, not in a book, but carved in a tall cedar totem pole in front of a chief's lodge:

Long ago, Raven, who had the power to change into human form, went fishing with his two slaves, Gitsaqeq and Gitsanuk. In those days they caught only spiny fish known as bullheads.

As they paddled, they became lost in a thick white blanket of cool smoke that closed around them. Unexpectedly, a mysterious woman emerged from the mist and sat in their canoe. Borrowing Raven's hat, she held it above her head and captured all the fog in it, allowing the sun to shine so that they were able to return to their camp. Raven fell in love with the magical Fog Woman and immediately married her.

One day when Raven and Gitsaqeq had gone fishing, his new wife and Gitsanuk became hungry. Fog Woman told the slave to bring her a container of water and, after she had dipped her finger in the liquid, she ordered Gitsanuk to face the sea and pour the water into a pool. The amazed servant discovered a large sockeye salmon in the pool.

BIRD DANCER

They cooked and ate the delicious new fish, but Fog Woman warned the slaves not to tell her husband about it. However, when Raven returned, he noticed a small piece of fish caught between Gitsanuk's teeth and forced the frightened slave to explain where it come from.

Raven then insisted that his wife prove her secret power. He filled his hat with water and Fog Woman dipped four fingers into it. When he emptied it, four fat salmon flopped onto the ground. After a filling meal, Fog Woman told Raven to bring her a bowl of water from a nearby spring. She washed her hands in the water, and when it was emptied back into the spring, suddenly there were numerous crimson salmon swimming in the clear waters.

TLINGLIT CANOE

The greedy Raven then forced his reluctant wife to make more and more salmon, until his smokehouse was overflowing with drying fish. Still he wanted more, but Fog Woman refused. Flinging her hair back, she made a wild motion, and a strange sound like the wailing wind came from the smokehouse growing louder and louder.

The angry Raven tried to grab his wife, but she slipped between his fingers like a wisp of fog and disappeared forever into the sea. All the salmon followed her. Only the bullheads were left in Raven's smokehouse.

Fog Woman, along with her daughter, Creek Woman, now live at the head of the river, and once a year they bring back the salmon.

Totem Tribes

In all the world, only the natives on the west coast of Canada belonged to totem clans. They lived in large one-room cedar lodges that housed forty to sixty people, and erected tall majestic totem poles, which were carved with visual stories of their family histories. Sometimes the entrance to the home was a doorway cut through the base of a thick totem pole. The clan or family emblem at the top of the pole would be a creature such as an eagle, mountain goat, killer whale, wolf, or grizzly bear. Some of the tribes of the Pacific were the Tlingit, Haida, Tsimshian, Bella Coola, Kwakiut, Nootka, and Coast Salish. Each had unique customs and cultures. For example, the Nootka were whalers who ventured into the ocean in large thirty-man canoes, while the Tlingit were known for making decorated chilkat blankets and capes that were said to have magical powers.

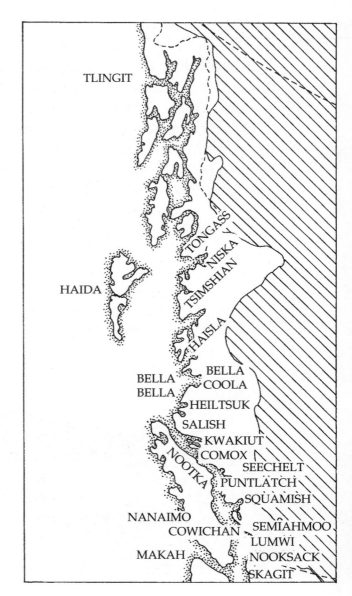

The Totem Story

The legend of Raven and Fog Woman would have appeared as follows on a totem. At the top of the pole would be carved the emblem of the chief who owned the story; in this case, the mythical mountain bird known as Kadjuk, who was brown with black-tipped wings. Below Kadjuk would be a blank space representing the open skies where the bird flew. Beneath these, the myth would begin with two bird figures symbolizing the slaves Gitsaqeq and Gitsanuk. Under them would be Raven, and finally would come Fog Woman holding two salmon.

Animal Magic

West Coast tribes believed that animals had magic powers to help or punish people and that they could transform themselves into human form.

Potlatch

When a newly carved totem pole was to be erected, the clan's chief would throw a large party known as a potlatch and invite all the other clans. Potlatch meant "gift," and it was the custom to give presents to all the guests. Gifts could be blankets, canoes, jewelry, clothing, weapons, or sometimes even slaves. The chief who gave away the most expensive articles was considered the most powerful. The guests were expected to have their own potlatches and return the favour.

Create a Family Totem

What You Need:
something shaped like a totem — a toilet paper roll or a taller roll
    from disposable paper towels
paints, markers, or crayons

What to Do:

1. Decide on an animal, bird, or fish that will be your family emblem. Draw, paint, or paste a picture (cut or photocopied from a magazine or book) of the creature at the top of your totem pole.

2. Think of an adventure that you or a family member has experienced, e.g., a trip, your first paying job, or a sports contest.

3. Choose some pictures that you can use to show the story. Paste or draw the visuals on your totem, beneath the family emblem.

4. Once your totem is complete, invite your friends or classmates to a potlatch. Present your totem and explain the visual story.

5. Think of a gift that you can offer to your guests. For example, food — cookies, cake, juices — or jewelry — hand-made rings, bracelets, or pendants (be imaginative, create them from bottle caps, straws, ribbons, etc.)

6. Of course, your friends will have to invite you to a potlatch in return and offer you a gift. Maybe you can all show your totems, tell your stories, and present your gifts at one large potlatch held on the same day.

NOOTKA FISHERMAN

Make a Makah Bird Mask

The peoples of the West Coast made colourful masks and wore them during ritual dances and other ceremonial occasions. Birds were very important in their cultures and were often used as subjects for masks.

What You Need:
scissors and a craft or X-Acto knife
white glue such as Elmer's
a blunt-edged tool, such as a table knife, for scoring tabs
a piece of string or yarn about 30 cm long
a red crayon or coloured pencil

What to Do*:
1. Colour the face and beak pieces. Do not colour the tabs.

2. Cut out the face and beak pieces. Cut out the black centres of the eyes.

3. Apply glue to the tab in the middle of the beak and attach it to the adjoining side.

4. Apply glue to the tabs around the beak and glue them in place behind the face piece.

5. Punch holes in the sides of the mask and attach a string.

*You may photocopy or trace these mask pages.

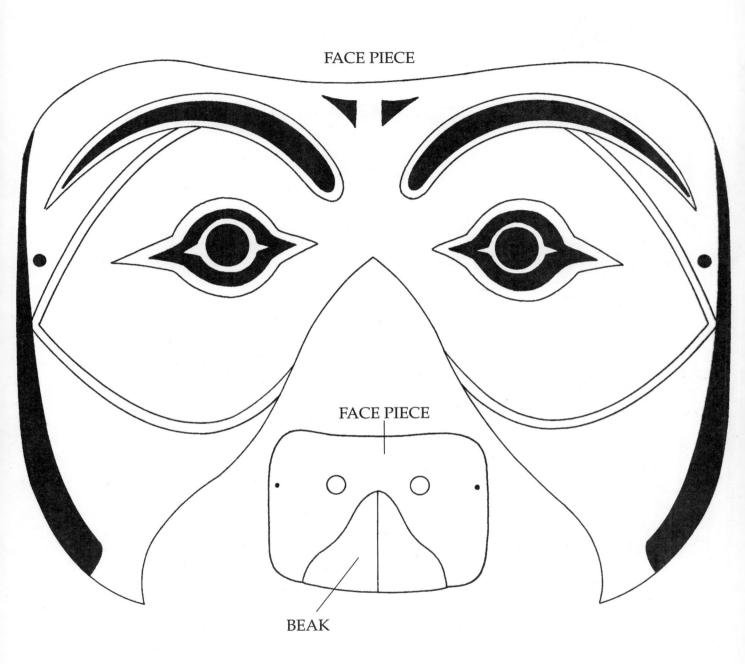

FACE PIECE

FACE PIECE

BEAK

85

CUT OUT FROM OTHER SIDE

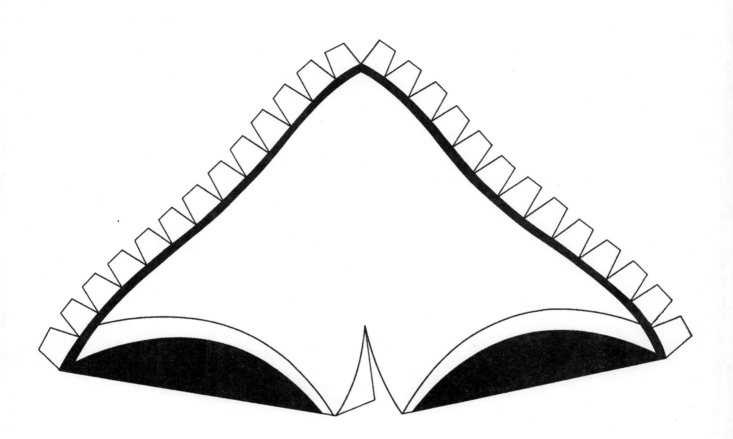

BEAK PIECE

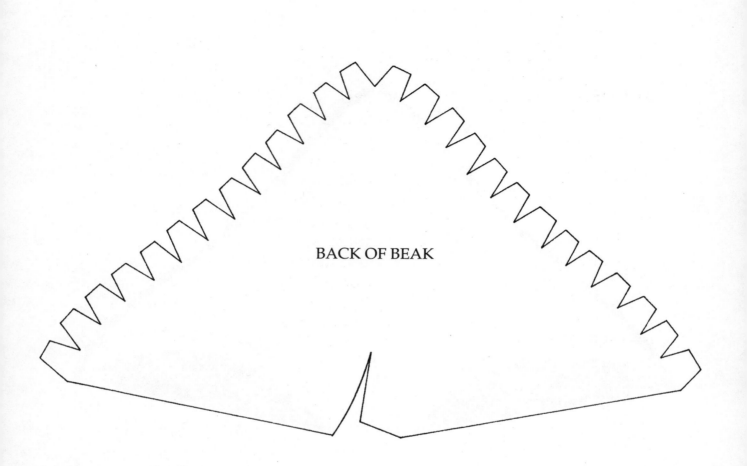

BACK OF BEAK

Answers to Native Peoples Crossword Puzzle, page 73:

ACROSS
2. Four
4. Naskapi
5. Sleeps
8. Potlatch
10. Wabanaki
11. Shaman
12. Vision
13. Beothuks
15. Dog
17. Mohawk
18. Teepee
19. Tokhonon
21. Igloos
23. Nuglukutug
25. Windigo
26. Salmon
27. Kayak
30. Mamateek
31. Hiawatha
32. Clans

DOWN
1. Wampum
3. Uktamkoo
6. Longhouses
7. Eskimos
9. Tawiskarong
13. Buffalo
14. Totems
15. Deganawidah
16. Iroquois
20. Tijuskeha
22. Glooscap
24. Umiak
28. Asia
29. Raven

Answer to Plains sign language question, page 62:

Index